FOCUS ON THE FAMILY ®

HELP!
MY SPOUSE AND I ARE DRIFTING APART

HELP!
MY SPOUSE AND I ARE DRIFTING APART

dr. bill maier
general editor

mitch temple
author

Tyndale House Publishers, Inc.
Carol Stream, Illinois

Editor: Brandy Bruce
Cover photograph © Mike Kemp/Getty Images. All rights reserved.
Cover design: Joseph Sapulich

Library of Congress Cataloging-in-Publication Data
Temple, Mitch, 1962-
  Help! My spouse and I are drifting apart / general editor, Bill Maier ;
author, Mitch Temple.
    p. cm.
  ISBN-13: 978-1-58997-457-9
  ISBN-10: 1-58997-457-3
  1. Marriage. 2. Intimacy (Psychology) 3. Couples—Psychology. I. Maier,
Bill. II. Title.
  HQ734.T27 2007
  646.7'8—dc22

                                        2007025797

Printed in the United States of America
1 2 3 4 5 6 7 8 9 /13 12 11 10 09 08 07

Contents

Foreword

Has the spark gone out in your marriage?
Are hugging, kissing, and sexual intimacy
relics of the ancient past? Could your marriage be characterized by the title of the old
Righteous Brothers song, "You've Lost That
Lovin' Feelin'"? If so, you've picked up
the right book. If your *spouse* gave this
book to you to read, resist the urge to get
defensive—instead, be thankful that he or
she cares enough about your relationship
to work on it.

My friend Mitch Temple, the director of
Focus on the Family's marriage department,
has designed this easy-to-read book for
every couple who longs to regain the "lovin'
feelin'" they once shared. Mitch is a marriage and family therapist who has worked

with hundreds of couples—some of whom were convinced that their marriage was dead. Many of those marriages not only survived—today they are thriving with a renewed sense of healthy intimacy.

In this book, Mitch will help you assess the current state of your marriage and teach you practical strategies that can get your relationship back on track. He'll also help you understand that you're not alone, and that every marriage experiences a normal ebb and flow in the level of closeness and romantic passion.

I pray that God will grant you the strength and courage to persevere in your marriage, and that He will use this book to revive and rejuvenate your relationship!

Dr. Bill Maier
Vice President, Psychologist in Residence
Focus on the Family

Introduction

Shawn and Katie met during college and were immediately attracted to each other. Friendship quickly blossomed into romance. The young couple spent every waking hour together. They shared dreams and fears. They trusted each other, and they grew in intimacy. Each focused on being the person that made the other complete. There was no doubt about it, Shawn and Katie wanted to spend the rest of their lives together.

But within the first few years of marriage, "life" began to happen. Shawn's career as a consultant became more demanding. His boss decided that Shawn needed to be on the road three to five nights a week. Katie's career as a marketing manager took off. Late nights, travel, and overtime took their toll on the couple's ability to spend time together. Church activities, extended family, and new hobbies also stole precious time from their relationship. Sexual encounters became rare. Resentment began to set in on both sides because neither had time for the other. Stress moved into their lives, and arguments intensified. Blame was tossed back and forth. Communication occurred only when it was necessary to maintain the business of daily life.

Before they knew it, the closeness they'd once felt was gone. They missed one another but couldn't seem to find the time or energy to reconnect.

ɔ ɔ ɔ

Bart and Tammy were the proud parents of twins. They had prepared for the twins in all the normal ways: saving money; decorating the nursery; buying strollers, cribs, diapers, and bottles. But there was one factor they hadn't prepared for: the strain on their marriage. Like many young couples, they believed that having kids would bring them closer together. They hadn't anticipated sleepless nights, never-ending crying and nonstop demands from the twins, illnesses, and little or no time for cuddling, talking, or even sex.

Their marriage took the blows week by week. Soon Bart was frustrated and angry because he was—at best—third place in Tammy's time and affection. Tammy was frustrated and resentful because it seemed selfish for Bart to want more from her than she could give. She felt she had nothing left after caring for two infants day after day. The couple grew further and further apart.

ɔ ɔ ɔ

Charles and Debbie were reaching the "happy time" of their marriage. At least, that's what everyone told them. Their two boys were away at college. Charles's career was on coast, and Debbie had retired from clerking at the county courthouse. Suddenly, they had more time on their hands than they had experienced in over 20 years. The problem was that they no longer felt close to each other. For the past 20 years, the couple had put all their energy into their careers and their two boys—both good investments of time and energy. But now they realized that they had neglected their marriage.

The silence in the house was deafening because their children were gone and they had forgotten how to talk to each other. Sure, they talked about everyday ness, crisis, and children can cause the level of closeness to increase or decrease. The question is: Once you've grown apart, can intimacy be restored? The answer, without reservation, is yes! Generations of successful marriages have proved that you can restore closeness once it is gone. All marriages experience lost intimacy at one point or another. The key is to restore it once it falters.

Throughout this short book, we'll talk about the need for closeness in marriages, and we'll delve deeper into what real intimacy looks like. Together we'll look at those things that can rob your relationship of intimacy, and in doing so, I'll help you evaluate the root of why you feel that you and your spouse are drifting apart. And most important, I'll explain how to restore intimacy in your marriage.

Take heart. Your marriage *can* get back on track. Intimacy *can* be restored. It takes time and effort, but the results are worth it.

Part One

The Basic Need for Intimacy

Marriage is a complex system engineered to foster closeness. It is not designed to foster independence. This doesn't mean that those of us who are married should lose our identity as individuals, or that we should be completely dependent on our spouses. It simply means that marriage is designed to cultivate unity, oneness, and intimacy. Just as the body needs oxygen to remain healthy and survive, a marriage needs intimacy to thrive and last.

Some systems, such as communities or neighborhoods, can exist with minimal interaction between the people who live there. I know of people who have lived in the same subdivision for more than 20 years but know little about the people next door. While that may work for communities, marriages cannot be successful if spouses decide to simply coexist. Marriages like these are reduced to business partnerships, consisting of people who simply do what has to be done. Couples in this state often stay together for the sake of the kids, financial reasons, or because of strong spiritual beliefs. Yet the satisfaction level is very low. The husband and wife no longer find happiness and fulfillment within each other. Sexual interactions are rare.

Pain and resentment can flow like a rushing river in such marriages. There is no loneliness like that of a marriage that has grown cold. The tension, silence, and distance seem to be amplified with every passing moment.

Maybe that is exactly how you feel at this moment.

What Is Intimacy?

Just the word *intimacy* raises all kinds of confusing thoughts for many people. Some of us search desperately for intimacy, settling for the slightest semblance of closeness. Others avoid intimacy as they would germs. Others have been influenced by Hollywood's depiction of intimacy—the kind that manifests itself in wildly romantic fantasies. And still others have reduced their understanding of intimacy simply to "sex." But that doesn't change the fact that every person—male and female—needs to feel wanted and connected. We have been designed to be in close relationship with others.

Real intimacy is much more than a feeling that comes from showing the right kind of affection, sharing deep thoughts, or even having passionate sex. Bonds can be formed through each of these actions and emotions, but intimacy involves more. True intimacy is the genuine closeness and connection that brings and holds couples together— emotionally, spiritually, intellectually, and physically. It's an ongoing connection, a oneness that occurs over time. True intimacy involves experiencing life together—happy times, triumphs, and victories, but also times of deep grief, tragedies, and trials.

Love and intimacy are deeply connected. You can't have one without the other. You and your spouse may say that you love each other, but the truth is that love cannot be sustained without closeness. Intimacy involves becoming a trusted, dependable friend. Spouses must experience life together in such a way that they know they can depend on each other to do whatever it takes to meet each other's needs, including being willing to defend and even die for each other.

But what is love? Is it just a feeling? Is it just a bunch of romantic actions? The greatest definition of love is found in the Bible. Genuine love involves being patient and kind with each other, not being rude, selfish, or demanding to have your way. Real love means forgiving when it's hard, and then letting go instead of keeping a record of past mistakes (1 Corinthians 13). Love involves both the right kinds of emotions and the right kinds of actions. When couples abide by these practices, they can experience incredible closeness and intimacy in marriage. And if the right actions and emotions produce closeness, surely the opposite behavior will cause detachment.

The Truth About Marriage

Dr. David Olson, a leading marriage researcher, has based his research on working with thousands of couples. Of the many discoveries he's made, one of the most revealing is that the level of closeness a couple feels in marriage, even the most healthy marriages, changes with circumstances and time.

When a couple is first married, they are very connected, typically overly con-nected. (Think back to Shawn and Katie in the introduction.) Couples like this don't have a great deal of structure in their lives and typically spend all their free time together.

But as time passes, more structure is needed to compensate for careers and other activities, especially if the couple has children. (Bart and Tammy would fall into this category.) They are typically not as emotionally connected as before, but still close. Then, as life continues for the couple, things like financial difficulties, adolescent problems, illnesses, and stress all play major roles in how much intimacy a couple may retain.[1]

The same is true for empty nesters. Though most couples at this stage in life were probably very close at one time, over the years the majority of their energy was probably invested in raising kids and other demands, with little time spent on each other. Often when the children leave home, the silence and emptiness underline the fact that the couple is emotionally disconnected.

During times like the ones we've just mentioned, when couples seem furthest apart, they may begin to believe that their marriage has become something that is no longer good. But the truth is that no matter where the intimacy level is, marriage is still important. Even tired, sick, disconnected marriages are important enough to rebuild, repurpose, and restore. We all need reminding of that fact, especially when the spark has gone.

Perhaps you feel that the spark in your marriage has gone out. Consider this: Research shows that not only is there a behavioral component (action element) to intimacy in marriage, but actions are also tied to chemicals in the brain. When couples are dating, and even throughout the honeymoon stage, dopamine is produced at greater levels in the brain. Dopamine is one of the main chemicals responsible for strong feelings of passion and excitement. That's why dating couples and newlyweds often feel such a "high."

However, these high levels of excitement-producing chemicals begin to diminish over time. In fact, some experts suggest that if dopamine levels remained elevated for longer periods of time, they would eventually kill us. In other words, euphoric feelings are not meant to last forever.[2]

The studies go on to show that high levels of dopamine are naturally replaced with another chemical called oxytocin, which is often referred to as the "bonding" chemical. It is the same chemical found at high levels while a mother is nursing her baby. Research suggests that couples who spend time together, touch each other, hug, hold hands, affirm, and serve each other have high levels of this chemical. Oxytocin seems to help substantiate and complement deep intimacy and bonding in couples.[3]

So while the lost passion and closeness

in your marriage *can* be restored to a healthy, mutually satisfying level, the level of passion you experienced while "falling in love" may be somewhat less now than before. But that's okay.

Society and the media are not always helpful in this regard. For years, society embraced marriage as one of the most important institutions on earth. But now the culture seems to say that if you no longer feel close to your spouse, or if you are unhappy and your needs are not being met, then your marriage has failed and you should move on to someone who can fulfill your needs.

In spite of this shift in how our culture views marriage, research still verifies what society held true for years—marriage really is a good thing. Studies have shown that married couples often enjoy a healthier lifestyle and live longer because they tend to take better care of themselves, exercise more, and avoid risky or harmful behaviors more than single or divorced people do. They also usually enjoy more sexual satisfaction than couples who only cohabit. Additionally, married couples are able to pool their resources and typically enjoy higher economic success than singles. Research also shows that children thrive best in homes with both a mother and a father.[4]

The bottom line is that no matter what our culture says or how you may feel about your marriage right now, it's worth saving. Healthy changes *can* occur. Don't give up hope.

Hooked on a Feeling

Strife, stress, shattered expectations, and broken trust have a unique way of wounding hope-filled dreams and emotions, but we must remember that feelings can lead us in unhealthy directions.

In Colorado, where we live, it's very easy to get lost while driving. The streets and roads were not laid down to accommodate the incredible growth we've experienced. So for the first two to three months after moving here, I was lost most of the time.

I realized quickly that it's risky to rely on "hunches." The problem is that most streets around here don't end up where you expect or feel that they should. Because of the mountainous terrain, certain roads may twist and turn until you are miles from where you want to be. I spent multiple hours of frustrated driving trying to find my way because I felt, or assumed, that "this was the way to go."

After a couple of months, a friend pointed out that relying on assumptions around here will get you lost every time. He taught me a great tactic to find my bearings: I was told to simply look for the mountains; they're always west of where you are. So if I'm ever lost, I can test my feelings with a marker—the mountains. If I'm heading away from the mountains, I know I'm heading east, no matter what my hunches tell me.

The same is true with emotions in marriage. They may tell you that you married the wrong person, that you will never restore the spark you once had in your marriage, that you are no longer in love, or that you will never be able to trust your spouse again after he or she has hurt you so deeply.

But the truth is that both marriage and love are about much more than how you feel or whether you are happy. Understand that there will be good days and bad days. It's unrealistic to expect to feel happy and loving all the time. Remember that marriage is a commitment. When your feelings tell you that your marriage isn't worth the effort, think back to those vows you made to your spouse on your wedding day. Commitment means honoring our vows to each other when we don't feel like it, when we lose hope, when it's no longer exciting, when we are hurt, when we argue, and even when our spouse doesn't do his or her part.

For example, if I relied only on my feelings as a parent, I would have thrown in the towel years ago. At times, my teens have hurt me, ignored everything I taught them, and willfully rebelled. But I'm committed to them. I've never thought about giving up my role as a parent or giving up on my children.

I know that good times and hard times are both part of the parenting journey.

Please understand that while feelings are important and shouldn't be ignored, they can at times lead you away from truth. Even if your spouse has hurt you deeply, the truth is that it's possible for love and trust to be restored.

But neither should we be naive: Restoring intimacy is not going to happen simply by wishing or hoping it will. Like a body that is out of shape and weak, a marriage has to be fed properly and exercised in order to experience intimacy. You have to make changes in attitude, perceptions, and actions in order for intimacy to return.

I like the story of a farmer and his wife who were riding down a prairie road in their old Ford pickup. The farmer was driving and his wife was sitting on the passenger side on the bench seat. Eventually the wife broke the silence and asked, "Hon, why don't we sit together in this truck like we used to?" The farmer thought a minute or two and finally answered, "Well, I ain't moved."

In working with couples who are experiencing loss of intimacy, I often tell this story and ask, "Who has moved?" In other words, what were the things that you once did that you are no longer doing? What traditions, habits, words, and expressions have you stopped using? Or what attitudes and actions have you adopted that are unhealthy and harmful to the other person? Often the answer is that both individuals have moved. Maybe you have simply stopped doing things or saying things because you felt they were no longer necessary, but in reality, they are vital to the health of your marriage.

ᖇ ᖇ ᖇ

We've seen that intimacy in marriage
fluctuates with time and changing life
circumstances, and that feelings can
come and go. Stress is another factor that
affects the level of intimacy in a marriage. Our next section will look specifi-
cally at stress in marriage and what you
can do about it.

Stress and Marriage

There are two general types of stress: short-term and long-term. If you lose your car keys, you may get frustrated and even angry, but once you find your keys, the stress will typically go away. If a car pulls out in front of you, you may experience anger, frustration, or fear, but only temporarily. That's short-term stress.

Long-term stress is more serious and requires more attention and help. This form of stress is present every day and can affect your emotional, physical, and relational health. People who live in a chronic state of stress often become depressed, moody, on edge, possibly even suicidal, and may eventually develop serious physical conditions such as heart disease, strokes, or cancer.

If chronic stress can have this effect

on the human body, imagine what it can do to a marriage. What would happen if you left the lights on inside your car for a couple of days? At first, the battery will be able to carry the load. But without recharging, the small lights will slowly drain the battery until it is dead. In the same way, stress will drain the intimacy from a marriage.

How Stress Affects Intimacy

The four most common stressors in marriages today have to do with finances, extended family, work-related issues, and losses. Other stressors include emotional difficulties; sexual difficulties; major purchases, such as buying a home; medical expenses; changing jobs; illnesses; and death in the family.[5] Issues such as infertility can also be huge stressors and drain intimacy.

Here are some specific ways stress can affect your marriage directly and indirectly:

- Stress can create additional conflict.
- Stress can heighten frustration, anger, and resentment.
- Stress can increase anxiety.
- Stress can cause chronic tension in the home.
- Stress can create a lack of sexual interest or sexual performance problems.
- Stress can cause depression.

Feelings of anxiety, frustration, distraction, anger, depression, and hopelessness can leave couples extremely disconnected. Children are very quick to sense stress and conflict and often act out or withdraw, causing an added dimension to problems in the marriage. Naturally, as more stress builds up in a marriage, intimacy will continue to fade.

Simple Things You Can Do to Relieve Stress

Now that we have seen how stress can affect intimacy, what can you do to work on this area in your marriage? Below I've listed a number of practical stress relievers.

1. *Exercise*. Start walking up to five days a week, briskly. Walk alone or walk together. Maybe push the stroller down to the park or walk around the neighborhood in the evening. If neither of you enjoys taking walks, find another outlet you can enjoy, such as biking or swimming. The point is to release some pent-up energy and emotion.

2. *Sleep*. Go to bed together. Don't stay up watching TV or working on the computer. Go to bed even if the tension is a little high. Just being together can be helpful, and getting the rest you need can

help you maintain energy and function better.

3. *Eat properly*. Don't skip breakfast or lunch. Not eating properly can throw the body out of balance and add more stress. Reassess your diet and consider areas where you may need to make healthful changes for you and your family.

4. *Drink water*. Many Americans walk around dehydrated. A dehydrated body will be more prone to stress.

5. *Relax*. Learn to take deep, cleansing breaths on a regular basis throughout the day. Clearing your lungs often lends itself to clearing the mind. You might ask your doctor for specific breathing techniques or look online at a Web site such as www.webmd.com or www.hhs.gov (United States Department of Health and Human Services) for steps and advice regarding breathing properly.

6. *Play*. Take up a hobby together such as bowling, golf, gardening, and so on.

Experience tells us that oftentimes when a stressor is removed or properly managed, satisfaction and closeness will return to the marriage. For example, when financial issues and strains are overcome with more income, debt repayment, or modified spending habits, the reduced stress allows most couples to refocus their attention and energy back on each other. Couples with small children or adolescents often feel considerably less stress in their marriage when their kids start to become more independent.

But how do you deal with stress while in the middle of pressing life issues, such as careers, children, in-law difficulties, or elder care? There are no easy answers to stress. If the stress you or your spouse is experiencing is chronic in nature, you may need to seek outside help. An outsider with a clear perspective can shed light on your situation. You might attend a stress management class offered through your employer, your place of worship, or a local hospital or mental health center.

If the stress in your life and marriage is less threatening and overwhelming, here is a simple four-step solution:

1. *Admit it.* Ignoring stress is like trying to push a balloon under water: It keeps popping up. If you can't identify what is causing stress in your life, consider taking a stress test, which can be administered by a counselor or your local mental health agency. You may also find a stress test online. If you discover that you score high on the stress scale, you should see a medical doctor to assess

your physical health as well as a counselor to assess your mental health and
treatment options.

2. *Talk about it.* If possible, don't try to
solve the problem without your spouse.
Oftentimes the simple act of asking for
help can provide a great deal of connection in a marriage. If your spouse is willing to open up about the stress in his or
her own life, don't browbeat, shame, or
judge him or her by saying such things
as, "That's nothing! You shouldn't let that
bother you. Get over it." Instead, take a
team approach: "We will work together
to find a solution."

3. *Manage it.* You can't always get rid
of those things that cause stress in your
marriage (such as jobs or children), but
you can learn new ways to manage the
stressors. We've mentioned practical
things you can do to help ease some

stress, such as exercising, going to bed earlier, and eating healthy foods. You might also begin spending a few moments every day to meditate and pray. Maybe you'd benefit from writing your feelings in a journal.

Evaluating your current time management strategy may lead to finding new, positive ways to incorporate personal time and time with your spouse into your schedule. For a stressed-out mom, an hour to herself in the evening might make all the difference in how she responds to her husband and children during the day. For a stressed-out dad, maybe allotting half an hour for personal time when he gets home from work can give him the boost he needs to spend positive time with the family during the evening. Smart tactics like these can go a long way in not only reducing stress but also feeling that you care about each other's needs.

4. *Solve it.* If your job continues to be a major source of stress in your home and marriage, maybe it's time to change jobs. If you can't change jobs, maybe you can speak with a supervisor regarding specific issues that are causing you the most stress, such as having to consistently work overtime, traveling too much, or having no administrative help.

If finances are causing strain in your marriage, seek financial counsel and make lifestyle changes. You might find a free financial analysis available online. Or a financial counselor might help you develop a budget. Be willing to make the hard decisions. Take action. Your mental, emotional, and physical health are worth it.

Part Three

Restoring
Intimacy

In the introduction I mentioned that my wife, Rhonda, and I found ourselves feeling disconnected early in our marriage. When that happened, we recognized that we couldn't change the stage of life we were in, but we also understood that we needed to get creative and smart about bringing back what we'd lost in our marriage. We committed to steer our marriage back toward closeness.

We started by developing a reconnection plan that included waking up a few minutes before the kids typically did and sitting together with a cup of coffee. We also committed to hiring a babysitter once every two weeks while we enjoyed time at our favorite restaurant. Once a month we asked a relative to allow the kids to stay over while we spent the night alone. Unexpected challenges arose from time to time that knocked us off this track, but we committed to getting back on. It wasn't easy, but with effort and determination, we were able to steer our marriage in a healthier direction. And you can too.

The Characteristics of Intimacy

So where do you start? By understanding and recognizing the characteristics of true intimacy, you can begin to make the changes needed for restoring closeness and rebuilding your relationship.

What does authentic intimacy look like? I've outlined some characteristics of couples who experience and maintain a close connection. Don't panic if you read over the list below and realize that you have few of these qualities in your marriage. You may not have any. That's okay. As we've seen, even the strongest, most successful marriages go through periods of intimacy drought. As you read over the list, consider the areas in your marriage where *you* can begin to make changes, regardless of your spouse's cooperation or lack thereof.

1. *Kindness.* Being rude to one another is a sure way to cause a disconnect in a marriage. One of the first things that I ask a wife who feels her husband is drifting away emotionally or physically is to start doing an unexpected act of kindness for him every day. No matter what he does, be kind. Inevitably, a shift from criticism to kindness will change the atmosphere, attitudes, and direction of a marriage. And showing kindness regardless of whether your spouse deserves it can take the sting out of a hurtful marriage and build a bridge back to your mate.

2. *Trust.* Do you trust your spouse? Can he or she trust you? Trust is knowing that we can depend on each other and that we will put forth our best effort toward honoring, protecting, and strengthening our marriage. It's knowing that our mate will not hurt us or our relationship intentionally. In healthy marriages, we may hurt our spouses unintentionally, but in most cases this isn't malicious. However, if you are in a marriage where your spouse is intentionally hurting you—emotionally or physically—or if trust has been broken by infidelity or pornography, you should seek professional counseling to help you deal with those serious issues.

3. *Understanding.* Understanding your spouse leads to acceptance. We are not flawless, perfect beings; we are human and we all have flaws. *Acceptance* means

not expecting your spouse to transform into someone he or she cannot be. The fact is that you can't change other people—the only changes that can precipitate positive change in your mate are the changes you make to yourself.

Let me state that understanding and accepting your mate does not mean never striving to make changes that will improve your relationship. While you may not be able to change deep personality-driven behaviors, such as introversion or extroversion, there usually *are* areas where you can make changes to improve your relationship. For example, maybe your wife is hurt that you don't listen more intently. Your willingness to do this could result in your wife in turn becoming more caring and attentive.

Maybe you have a habit of approaching every discussion with your spouse defensively. Even if it's not easy, this is an area where you could make changes. If a husband recognizes that he begins most discussions angrily, shaking his finger, or if a wife realizes that she often interrupts her husband, they can commit to making communication changes that foster resolution. One important change like this can lead to additional big wins for couples. It demonstrates that with effort and determination they can succeed, which provides motivation to make changes in other areas.

4. *Concern for the other*. Concern means caring about your spouse's well-being—emotionally, physically, and spiritually. This requires you to know what is really going on in his or her everyday world. You must also show a willingness to engage in his or her thoughts, feelings, fears, and daily activi-

ties. Showing genuine concern can often begin with a simple question: "You mentioned you were not feeling good about your job yesterday. How did things go today?" and then truly listening to the answer.

5. *Apologizing and forgiving.* We all make mistakes. Mistakes can bring us closer together or pull us further apart. If we acknowledge our mistakes, take responsibility, show sorrow for the hurt they caused, and make a concerted effort to change, then mistakes can lead to real connection and growth in a marriage. Offering a heartfelt and humble apology can be the first step to coming back together with the person you love. This works even when you don't feel you are the cause of the problem.

The truth is that it's almost impossible for a couple to argue without both people doing or saying something they regret. Start with what *you* did wrong. Offering an apology may often elicit an apology from your spouse.

Forgiveness is the next step. This process needs to be practiced daily. Forgiveness is a willingness to let go of past hurts. It *doesn't* mean forgetting what was said or done, it simply means letting go of it. Don't allow what happened to stand in the way of how you feel toward your spouse any longer.

Some hurts are deeper than others, though, so forgiveness can be more difficult in some situations than others. For example, it's less complicated to forgive a spouse who hurt your feelings by saying something unkind versus a spouse who has been unfaithful. Yet both types of hurt can and must be forgiven eventually, whether you remain together or not. If you have experienced the deep wounds caused by adultery, abuse, or addiction in your marriage, then you will likely need professional help to direct you through the complicated process. But understand that everyday forgiveness is necessary to experience intimacy in a marriage, and it's worth the struggle to get there.

What Intimacy Is Not

I have told you what intimacy is; now let me touch on what it is *not*. Intimacy does *not* mean just doing one thing well. It involves many elements. For example, deeper intimacy is not produced by having better sex on a more regular basis. Though regular, healthy sex is an important factor in intimacy, it is not the only factor. Sex is often the natural expression of being intimately connected in heart, mind, and body.

As stated before, intimacy is built by doing, saying, and feeling the right things. Things such as showing mutual respect for each other, serving each other, appreciating each other, being trustworthy, and touching each other on a regular basis are all essential to healthy intimacy. Couples missing one or many of the above elements will simply not experience the same level of closeness as couples who incorporate them into their daily routine.

Some couples struggle with what an intimate, close marriage looks like even before they are married. Many people come from homes where their parents were extremely disconnected, had little time for each other, and communicated little. Conflict may have been a normal reality in their homes. As a result, when these individuals become adults and get married, they bring a number of distorted perceptions into their marriage. Maybe this describes your background. It does for many couples today.

Distorted perceptions, negative experiences, stress, and other challenges in marriages often lead to intimacy problems, which range from minor to major. When couples come to me for help because they have drifted apart, I recommend that they separately make a list of five things that they used to do early in their marriage that they no longer do. Ironically, most of the time their lists are similar. I then give them the remedy for their disconnectedness: Start doing these things again. Simple? Absolutely. Does it work? Absolutely. If it is impossible for a couple to do all five, then I encourage them to start with one. Try making a list of your own.

For example, if small talk after dinner each evening was one of the things that brought you and your spouse together in the beginning, begin spending 10 minutes talking while cooking dinner in the kitchen. Bringing back this one element can be the beginning of reconnecting in your marriage. Maybe you used to leave love notes for each other or call each other during the day.

The old axiom that if you do what you have always done, then you will get the same result, is true. The only way to get different results is to start doing something different. To expect to foster intimacy when you are repeating the same bad behaviors is unrealistic. You must bring back the attitudes and actions that worked before, or incorporate new, healthy practices into your marriage.

If you can't remember what you used

to do before, look for ways to refresh your memory like looking through wedding pictures, dating pictures, pictures of the first few years of your marriage; reading old love letters; or asking friends and family to recall things you once did but are no longer doing.

For some couples, life circumstances may have changed drastically since their early days as a married couple. You may now have a household of children or even elderly parents living at home. Incorporating new practices into your schedule can provide a jump start to your marriage. For example, an empty-nest couple might decide to take a cruise together or take dance lessons. A couple with children in the home could try setting aside time for a coffee or dessert date once a week, like Rhonda and I did. Also, reserving time to spend with other couples in similar life stages can provide an avenue for support and friendship.

Next, we'll take a look at certain behaviors and habits that can steal the intimacy from your marriage.

Thieves of Intimacy

Ben was pulling into the driveway as his cell phone rang. He knew it was Mandie, his wife, wondering where he was and why he wasn't home yet. He slowed his steps as he neared the front door. Mandie came rushing around the corner as he made his way through the entry, instantly handing him their nine-month-old daughter and drilling him on why he was five minutes late. His twin five-year-old sons were tugging at his jacket. Mandie was, once again, reminding him that she had been home all day with the kids and now needed his help. Exhaustion and annoyance exploded in Ben as he accused Mandie of being selfish and never considering how much stress he was under at work. Mandie lashed back that he never helped her with the children. As the tension rose, the baby began to cry and both boys started misbehaving, accidentally knocking over a vase. Within moments, Mandie and Ben's frustration was diverted to the kids. Now upset with each other and the children, Ben stormed out of the room, and Mandie held her head in her hands and cried.

Negative reactions and destructive habits like the ones Ben and Mandie displayed can rob relationships of vital qualities needed to build healthy marriages. It's easy for good marriages to allow intimacy to slip away due to ignorance, lack of understanding, or unwillingness to recognize that a real problem has developed.

To help you better understand and identify things that may be robbing your marriage of intimacy, I've listed 10 common thieves of intimacy:

1. *Lack of patience.* A boss who expects you to perform with flawless perfection each and every day has very unrealistic expectations. No one wants a boss like that. The same is true of husbands and wives who overlook their own mistakes and yet emphasize and draw attention to their spouse's mistakes. No wife wants to hang out with, nor have sex with, a husband who is constantly pointing out that she messes up all the time. The same applies to a wife who constantly berates her husband.

2. *Selfishness.* Despite what TV ads tell us, it's not all about us. If a marriage is made up of an individual, or worse two individuals, who expect to have their way all the time, it's only a matter of time until a battle erupts. Moving from a "me

first" mentality to a sense of togetherness and unity demands that we must be willing to compromise.

If your spouse is the one who is exhibiting a selfish nature, sometimes a nonthreatening, sincere note can broach the topic. If he or she becomes obstinate and continues displaying extreme selfishness, it may be necessary to seek outside help from a pastor or spiritual mentor he or she respects. Ongoing selfish behavior can not only hurt your marriage but also other people, including your extended family (children, parents, siblings).

3. *Anger.* It's normal for spouses to do or say things that make each other angry. We all do this no matter how hard we try not to. Anger is a natural response, just like fear, joy, or anxiety. These emotions have a unique purpose and are part of being human. For example, fear can keep

us from getting too close to a dangerous cliff. Anxiety can prompt us to take action. But any emotion can become abnormal.

If one or both spouses experience anger on a regular or daily basis, something is wrong. Ongoing anger will destroy a marriage just as it will destroy your body. Out-of-control anger can be the first step toward physical abuse. If ongoing anger is an issue in your marriage, seek help with a professional. Even if your spouse is unwilling to go with you, counseling may help you learn how to manage your response to your spouse and help him or her receive the assistance he or she needs.

4. *Bringing up the past.* Bringing up past mistakes in a marriage is like throwing gasoline on a fire. It only reinforces previous hurts and opens new wounds.

Eventually you or your spouse will have had enough and overreact. Bringing up hurtful things our spouses did in the past is a signal that we have not let go of the hurt nor reached a place of forgiveness.

One spouse may be holding on to the past as a way of showing revenge, maintaining control of power, or making his or her spouse suffer. The problem with this approach is that it adds more pain to the situation and doesn't resolve anything. No matter how badly our spouse has hurt us, it's unhealthy to hold the past over his or her head and withhold forgiveness.

You may say that you have forgiven your spouse, but are your actions contradicting your words? If you have trouble letting go of the past, you may need to talk with someone outside your marriage (a counselor, mentor, or trusted friend) to help you discover why you can't let go and learn how to overcome those feelings. No amount of dedication, commitment, or verbal affirmations of love will easily counteract actions such as rehashing the past.

5. *Withholding affection or sex.* No matter how justified you may feel about withholding affection or sex, it's harmful. We are all hardwired to need physical affection and sexual satisfaction, though sometimes on different levels. To withhold affection or sex from your mate is not only unhealthy but also dangerous. When we willfully withhold something that was designed to be fulfilled in marriage, we put our partners in a situation where they may begin to look elsewhere for it. Please understand that withholding sex still doesn't justify committing adultery or viewing pornography. But with-

holding what rightfully belongs to the other causes frustration, anger, and resentment, and destroys closeness.

Instead of withholding something your spouse needs, practice healthier ways to let him or her know that your needs are not being met or that you've been hurt by the lack of affection. For example, if your husband failed to clean the garage as you requested and went golfing, instead of ignoring him or withholding sex, sit down and talk to him. Make him aware in a loving way how much his actions hurt you and how they made you feel. It's important to communicate your feelings without blaming or attacking the other person.

6. *Pornography.* Often pornography is justified by one spouse saying, "At least I haven't had sex with someone else." However, pornography can send the same

signals to a spouse as a physical affair, such as, "I am finding fulfillment with something or someone other than you." Most spouses feel some of the same feelings of hurt and betrayal as they do from a physical affair when they discover their partner has been viewing pornography.

Another factor that makes pornography hurtful is the secrecy involved. Pornography often destroys one of the vital components of marriage—trust. Judy may ask herself, *If Tom will do this, then what's to say he won't have a physical affair?* Pornography is also very addictive. It's a problem that will typically get worse and can lead to other unhealthy actions such as physical affairs. You may have to exercise tough love in order for your spouse to get the help that he or she really needs. See the resources section for more advice on this issue.

If you or your spouse has struggled with pornography use before, it's important for both of you to work together to set boundaries regarding time alone on the computer or in front of the television in order to avoid the temptation to view pornography. Talk together about ways to protect the intimacy in your marriage.

7. *Threatening divorce.* No matter how upset you become, you should not threaten divorce. When you threaten divorce, you weaken your level of commitment; you weaken how your spouse views your level of commitment; your threat is seen as manipulation, which causes more resentment and anger; and your spouse loses respect and trust for you because you are indicating that you are unwilling to stick it out.

If you have used the threat of divorce as a way to shock your spouse into reality about how disconnected or hurt you feel, you may need to apologize and let him or her know that you are willing to do whatever it takes to make the marriage better. Do this even if you feel that your spouse should be the one to make this statement and get help first. Your example and willingness can have a positive effect and possibly prompt your spouse to work on the problem with you.

8. *Unwillingness to change.* Every individual has desires and preferences, likes and dislikes. But when it comes to essentials of marriage, such as sex, affection, and mutual respect, we must learn how to facilitate and nurture these needs. These qualities are vital to the health and longevity of any marriage.

If you are not by nature a very sexual or affectionate person, reading books, attending marriage seminars, talking with more mature men or women (mentors), and even counseling can help you in these areas. As long as you say, "I'm just not a sexual or affectionate person," your spouse will interpret this as an unwillingness to change.

The same is true regarding respect. If you grew up in a home where your parents were disrespectful to each other, you may tend to follow the same unhealthy pattern. (You can see the recommended resources section for more materials concerning respect in marriage.) But a lack of respect in marriage is a sure way to further disconnect.

If your spouse is the one who makes excuses for not changing in these areas, let him or her know how it makes you feel by setting aside a private time to talk or by writing him or her a letter. Don't wait until you are upset or angry to talk to him or her about it. Remember, don't blame, attack, or speak down to your spouse; he or she will only become defensive. But don't procrastinate regarding these important issues.

9. *Lack of boundaries*. Time together, and especially time alone, is one of the most important factors in marriage. If your schedule has become so busy that you can't spend time with your spouse, you need to make adjustments. Even good things such as careers, church activities, volunteer efforts, hobbies, computer use, children's activities, and spending time with extended family can all become excessive and hurtful without boundaries.

Start developing healthy boundaries by sitting down with your spouse and evaluating your family schedule. Together you may be able to come up with creative ideas to free up time for each other. Time alone together may simply mean spending some time on the deck together, reading a book together, or taking a walk.

Maybe you need to look into babysitting co-ops or other inexpensive ways to find help with the children for an evening or afternoon. Perhaps you could commit to having at least one night a month reserved for the two of you. For those couples with young children, consider asking a relative or a responsible high-school student from your local church to stay with the kids.

The important thing is to get a regular time on your schedule. If you don't create and protect a relationship margin in your life, something will squeeze it out.

Sometimes the solution is simply learning to say *no* and cutting out some of the many activities families are involved in today. Though at first it may be difficult and may cause some initial hurt feelings with others, it is important to do. You can't control how others feel or respond; your main priority is to strengthen and protect your marriage. Let others know that because you need to spend more time together, you are making some changes regarding your schedule. Most people will eventually respect that decision. Don't be afraid to take this important step toward protecting your marriage.

10. *Previous marriage/stepfamily issues.* If you are in a second or third marriage, there are unique circumstances that will tend to pull you and your current spouse apart. Issues such as child-custody battles, visitation rights, discipline of your or your spouse's children, feeling left out

or second-rate compared to your spouse's children, and dealing with ex-spouses can create stress, hurt, and division in your current marriage.

If some of these concerns are causing you to feel disconnected and are interfering in your marriage, talk about them with your spouse. If the problem is so complex that the two of you can't solve it on your own, go to a family counselor who is experienced in stepfamily issues. You might join a support group together for encouragement and advice. Try to keep your spouse involved in the decision process as much as possible. Don't keep anything from your spouse, even if you think that by withholding information you are protecting him or her. Keeping things from one another will only cause mistrust and hurt.

Couples who learn to protect their

marriage by educating themselves, cooperating, and communicating openly have a stronger chance of weathering the stepfamily storms that will arise.

ꝺ ꝺ ꝺ

We've looked at different ways to reconnect in marriage, such as reducing stress, bringing back behaviors that worked before, incorporating healthier practices into marriage, and avoiding the thieves of intimacy. But let's talk about a few more specific steps to take if you and your spouse are drifting apart.

Steps to Restoring Intimacy

1. *Commit to making a change.* Do you remember when you were a child and you did things that were frustrating to your mom such as popping your leg with a pencil during church? If you continued

doing so after she asked you to stop, she would eventually grab the pencil out of your hand and say firmly, "Just stop it!" Sometimes the principle of "just stop it" applies to husbands and wives too. An issue may be minor, and yet if it is something that a couple says or does over and over, it may be time to stop doing it. No matter who seems to instigate or perpetuate it, and even if "your parents did it," you must stop any behavior that causes division in your marriage.

This doesn't mean that you will not occasionally relapse into old habits. It means that one of you, and eventually both of you, have to commit to making changes in your attitude and behavior. Because some habits are so ingrained that you can't stop them on your own, you may need the help of a counselor who is trained to address out-of-control

behaviors. Or you might confide in a
trusted friend and ask him or her to help
keep you accountable for your words and
actions. But most important, you must
be willing to commit to stopping those
harmful behaviors that are causing tension or distance between you and your
spouse.

2. *Serve each other*. Serving your
spouse and doing things that he or she
appreciates sends the signal that "I care
about you . . . I am interested in you . . .
I want to make your life easier . . . I want
to make you happy . . . and I love you."

Couples who serve one another build
up a great deal of emotional equity in
their relationship so that when hurts,
stresses, or crises occur, the equity from
previous good deeds can be drawn down.

Acts of service in a marriage will look
different for each couple. A husband and

wife might trade off cleaning the kitchen after dinner every night. One spouse might watch the kids one night a week so his or her mate can join a book club or take an online class.

Spouses don't always automatically know what acts of service their mate would appreciate most. Talk openly together about this subject. Perhaps the two of you could each write up a short list of those things that would make a difference in your life. Make an effort to do at least one unexpected act of service for your spouse every week.

I have witnessed deeply troubled marriages turn completely around simply by directing couples to develop the habit of serving one another. Learn to do things that build your spouse up, even when you don't feel like it. We do things at our jobs every day that we don't feel like doing, possibly for complete strangers, so why can't we do the same for the one we love? Serving your mate is a worthwhile investment in your marriage.

3. *Learn to listen.* We hear, but we don't always listen. Some levels of listening are for practical reasons such as direction or instruction: When your spouse asks you to carry the dirty clothes to the laundry room, your affirmative response indicates that you listened. But the kind of listening that builds intimacy involves really connecting and genuinely trying to understand where your spouse is coming from. When your spouse shares a concern or a problem, or just had a bad day, he or she may not necessarily want you to offer solutions or analyze the situation. Your mate might just need you to listen. Effective listening is something you have to be intentional

about and something that most people have to learn to do.

The next time your spouse attempts to share something with you, try to follow these steps: 1. Establish eye contact. 2. Don't allow other things to distract you while your spouse is speaking. Stay focused on what your spouse is saying. 3. Don't think of how you will respond—just listen.

If your spouse is the one who does not listen well, share these three guidelines as suggestions, not mandates. Then begin by modeling effective listening yourself. Make intimate listening a priority in your marriage.

4. *Communicate honestly*. Like listening, communicating on a deep level takes intentional work and practice. You may be fully aware of what you are trying to communicate to your spouse. But make

sure to always ask your spouse to clarify what he or she heard you say. That way you can be sure that what you intended to communicate is what you actually communicated. If necessary, take time to repeat yourself, possibly using different words or by offering an example.

Also, be careful what you are communicating through your body language (also known as secondary communication). Your lips may be saying one thing while your body language is communicating just the opposite. Negative body language can have an overriding and confusing effect on a listener. Make sure that what you are saying with your body aligns with what you are feeling.

And most important, speak the truth. Dishonesty is one of the quickest ways to destroy intimacy. When you lie, whether big or small, you destroy trust. And building back broken trust in a marriage is extremely difficult. So when tempted to stretch the truth a little, think about the long-term effects your decision could have on your marriage.

5. *Protect your marriage.* No matter how bored or dissatisfied you may feel in your marriage, it's crucial that you set boundaries with opposite-sex friendships. Husbands and wives who feel unfulfilled and unhappy are extremely vulnerable to emotional and physical affairs. For a person who wishes his or her mate was more attentive, chatting online with a stranger can quickly develop into something more serious. For a husband or wife who feels frustrated at home, a seemingly innocent friendship with a coworker can spiral into an affair.

You might need to commit to not

sharing intimate details of your marriage with someone other than your spouse or a counselor. Maybe you need to avoid visiting chat rooms or having extended phone calls or lunch dates alone with a member of the opposite sex. Evaluate your behavior and dress attire. Have you been unintentionally flirtatious or dressing provocatively in the workplace?

Realize also that romance novels, soap operas, and movies with overt sexual themes can have a negative effect on your marriage. Rather than foster intimacy, these unrealistic depictions of love and romance can cause discontent in your relationship. Having an accountability partner when it comes to your Internet use, steering clear of harmful books or movies, avoiding business travel alone with a colleague of the opposite sex, and being aware of your own emotional weaknesses are just a few ways you can be proactive about protecting your marriage.

6. *Remember that sex starts first thing in the morning (build up to it)*. Sex is more complex than we may think. We often think of it as solely a physical act, but it's a mental and emotional process as well. This is why we don't typically want to have sex with our spouse while there is unresolved conflict between us. We need to feel a certain level of connection and closeness before sex can be completely satisfying. Sex should be an extension of treating each other with respect and affection and having the right kinds of emotion toward each other. The best sex usually culminates from what has been building throughout the day.

7. *Make changes in appearance and habits*. Compare recent photographs of yourself to early ones. Have you gained a

great deal of weight? Have you lost a great deal of weight? Have you stopped exercising? Are you as concerned about what you wear around the house as you used to be?

Remember that physical attraction was probably a major component of what brought you and your spouse together. If you have lost some closeness with your spouse, a good place to start rebuilding that connection might be your appearance. Ask a close friend to help evaluate your looks. Try a new hairstyle. Change those old glasses to a more modern style. Visit your local discount clothing store. Don't be afraid to ask store employees for their opinion on what looks good on you.

If you think your spouse needs to make changes in this area, start with yourself. Your changes will likely encourage him or her to make positive changes in how he or she looks. Also, consider any habits you may have picked up since being married, such as throwing dirty clothes on the floor, smoking, dipping, watching TV for hours at a time, and so on. Annoying habits can chip away at the intimacy we feel for each other.

Your ability to recognize a habit and your willingness to change can go a long way toward getting your mate's attention. Let him or her know that you are making the effort because you want to become the best person you can be for your spouse. Don't try to change everything, just start small, but start. One victory can lead to another.

A Word of Caution

For some people, taking the advice this book offers may be enough to jump start a marriage that needs help. For others who feel a stronger disconnect and have already tried making changes on their own, attending marriage retreats can be a good way to hear fresh perspective. Asking another, older couple whom you respect to mentor you can also be a positive way to gain valuable advice and encouragement. However, if you or your spouse would be more comfortable talking with a professional rather than a mentor, trusted friend, or even a pastor, look into meeting with a counselor.

Not every couple can get back on track without outside help. Some marriages have grown so far apart and carry such deep wounds that they need others to help steer them in the right direction. Some marriages are plagued with addictions or abuse. If physical abuse is occurring in your marriage, you need to seek safety and professional help immediately.

You can contact the Focus on the
Family counseling department at 719-
531-3400, extension 7700, between the
hours of 9:00 A.M. and 4:30 P.M. moun-
tain time, Monday through Friday, to
receive a confidential, one-time session
with one of our licensed counselors. If
more help is needed, we can refer you to
a counselor in your local area.

If you were having continuing chest
pains, wouldn't you seek help from a
medical doctor? Your heart is too important to ignore. Apply that same principle
to your relationships: If your marriage is
hurting and doesn't seem to be getting
better, isn't it important enough to go to
a relationship doctor for help? Don't let
anyone make you feel that there is something wrong with seeking help for your
marriage. In fact, it takes a great deal of
courage to face uncomfortable issues

rather than simply ignoring them, hoping they will go away.

Even if your spouse refuses to go to counseling with you, you should go. You may receive insight on how to manage the situation, how to make personal changes, and how these changes can positively affect your spouse. Don't underestimate the value of seeking help on your own if your spouse is resistant.

ɔ ɔ ɔ

No couple intends to grow apart—life just happens and things end up that way. The good news is that though it will take intentionality, planning, perseverance, imagination, ingenuity, and faith, restoring intimacy can happen. If you and your spouse were in separate boats, canoeing down a stream together, and you started drifting apart, what would you do?

Panic? Complain? Argue? Just let it happen? Blame the problem on the rocks and turbulent water? Blame each other? No, you would make changes. You would put your paddles back in the water and start paddling toward each other. If you didn't, you would drift farther and farther apart.

In that same sense, restoring a relationship requires work and action. But the end result will be what you both really want: closeness, teamwork, and a lifetime of intimacy.

Notes

1. David H. Olson and Amy K. Olson, *Empowering Couples, Building on Your Strengths*, 2nd ed. (Minneapolis: Life Innovations, Inc., 2000), 91. Used with permission.

2. Helen E. Fisher, Arthur A. Ron, Debra Mashek, Haifan Li, and Lucy L. Brown, "Defining the Brain Systems of Lust, Romantic Attraction and Attachment," *Archives of Sexual Behavior*, 31, no. 5 (Academic Research Library, October 2002), 413.

3. Ibid.

4. Glenn Stanton, "Why Children Need Father-Love and Mother-Love," http://www.citizenlink.org/FOSI/

marriage/A000000993.cfm, August 29, 2003.

5. David H. Olson and John DeFrain, *Marriages & Families: Intimacy, Diversity, and Strengths*, 5th ed. (New York: McGraw Hill, 2006).

Resources

Desai, Amy. *Before You Divorce* (booklet). Available through Focus on the Family by request.

Dobson, Dr. James. *5 Essentials for Lifelong Intimacy* (Sisters, Ore.: Multnomah, 2005).

Dobson, Dr. James. *Love Must Be Tough: New Hope for Marriages in Crisis* (Sisters, Ore.: Multnomah, 2004).

Dobson, Dr. James. *Love for a Lifetime: Building a Marriage That Will Go the Distance* (Sisters, Ore.: Multnomah, 2004).

Eggerichs, Emerson. *Love and Respect* (Carol Stream, Ill.: Tyndale House Publishers/Focus on the Family, 2004).

Evans, Debra. *Blessing Your Husband* (Carol Stream, Ill.: Tyndale House Publishers/Focus on the Family, 2003).

Focus on the Family/Life Innovations Online Marriage Assessment. Go to http://go.family.org/couplecheckup/

Janssen, Al. *The Marriage Masterpiece* (Carol Stream, Ill.: Tyndale House Publishers/Focus on the Family, 2005).

Stephens, Steve. *Blueprints for a Solid Marriage* (Carol Stream, Ill.: Tyndale House Publishers/Focus on the Family, 2006).

Swihart, Phillip J. and Wilford Wooten. *Complete Guide to the First Five Years of Marriage* (Carol Stream, Ill.: Tyndale House Publishers/Focus on the Family, 2007).

Temple, Mitch. *When Your Marriage Needs Help* (booklet). Available through Focus on the Family by request.

Marriage and Conflict: Turning Disagreement into Growth (booklet). Available through Focus on the Family by request.

Trent, John. *Breaking the Cycle of Divorce* (Carol Stream, Ill.: Tyndale House Publishers/Focus on the Family, 2006).

Dr. Bill Maier is Focus on the Family's vice president and psychologist in residence. Dr. Maier received his master's and doctoral degrees from the Rosemead School of Psychology at Biola University in La Mirada, California. A child and family psychologist, Dr. Maier hosts the national television feature *Focus on Your Family with Dr. Bill Maier* and the national *Weekend Magazine* and *Family Minute with Dr. Bill Maier* radio programs. In addition, Dr. Maier is a media spokesperson for Focus on the Family on a variety of family-related issues. He and his wife, Lisa, have been married for more than seven years and have three children.

๑ ๑ ๑

Mitch Temple is a licensed marriage and family therapist. He holds two graduate degrees in ministry and marriage and family therapy from Southern Christian University. Mitch currently serves as the director of the marriage department at Focus on the Family in Colorado Springs, CO. He has conducted intensives nationwide for couples on the brink of divorce and has served as a family, pulpit, and counseling minister in churches for a total of 23 years. He served as director over a counseling center, pastoral care, small groups, and family ministry for a large church for 13 years. He and his wife, Rhonda, have been married for more than 24 years and have three children.

FOCUS ON THE FAMILY®

Welcome to the family!

Whether you purchased this book, borrowed it, or received it as a gift, we're glad you're reading it. It's just one of the many helpful, encouraging, and biblically based resources produced by Focus on the Family for people in all stages of life.

Focus began in 1977 with the vision of one man, Dr. James Dobson, a licensed psychologist and author of numerous best-selling books on marriage, parenting, and family. Alarmed by the societal, political, and economic pressures that were threatening the existence of the American family, Dr. Dobson founded Focus on the Family with one employee and a once-a-week radio broadcast aired on 36 stations.

Now an international organization reaching millions of people daily, Focus on the Family is dedicated to preserving values and strengthening and encouraging families through the life-changing message of Jesus Christ.

Focus on the Family Magazines

These faith-building, character-developing publications address the interests, issues, concerns, and challenges faced by every member of your family from preschool through the senior years.

| Focus on the Family **Citizen®** U.S. news issues | Focus on the Family **Clubhouse Jr.™** Ages 4 to 8 | Focus on the Family **Clubhouse™** Ages 8 to 12 | **Breakaway®** Teen guys | **Brio®** Teen girls 12 to 16 | **Brio & Beyond®** Teen girls 16 to 19 | **Plugged In®** Reviews movies, music, TV |

FOR MORE INFORMATION

 Online:
Log on to www.family.org
In Canada, log on to www.focusonthefamily.ca

 Phone:
Call toll free: (800) A-FAMILY (232-6459)
In Canada, call toll free: (800) 661-9800

BP06XFM